Author Freedom Guidebook

by Dr, Robert C. Worstell

**Online course and additional materials are available at
<u>http://livesensical.com/go/author-freedom/</u>**

Table of Contents

Who Else Wants to Write Bestsellers That Become Classics?

Get No-Charge Access to Writing and Publishing Materials from Our Library Collection

Instant Access - Join Here

Click or type into your browser:

http://livesensical.com/go/writingbooks/

0. Welcome to Your Freedom

When the vast majority of people on this planet say they have a book in them, but less than one percent ever publish it, that's a shame.

Worse, far less than one percent of *those* ever make a living from writing and publishing.

It's no small wonder why authors are held with such respect and even awe.

The trick is that any one and everyone can write and publish and make a decent living these days. And that's been possible for almost a decade at this point.

What we are about to cover in this course is a set of materials which are the basics. They dispell some misconceptions and downright lies which are being spread. The people who do this make more money from you if you keep your day job and just pay them.

Of course, you are reading this because you don't really believe them.

And that is a good thing. Because you are expected to question and test everything you read, hear, or experience during this course. The acid test is that it has to work for you to be useful.

We've also included practical steps for you to apply, as well as the transcripts and additional downloads for each lesson. If you want, it's also being published as an ebook, so you can study on your smartphone or other device any time you want.

While these lessons are best studied in sequence, after you complete the first one and publish a book of your own (in just 30 minutes, for free) then you can study the rest anyway you want. It's just key that you get your first book done and out of the way.

Are you ready to get more freedom into your life?

Then let's get started.

1. Get Published

– Become a Published Author in about 30 minutes.

The First Lie Fed to Authors: It Takes Lots Of Time And Money To Get Your Writing Published.

The truth is: a minimum viable book can be published in a single day or just a morning or an afternoon.

And it costs you nothing butyour time.

Most people think writing and publishing is incredibly hard and difficult and expensive.

Writing is simple – and free.

You sit down and write until you're done, or do it over several days.

Publishing is also simple – and free:

- You need 2500 words.
- You need a cover.
- You need 50 characters of a description.

Writing

Find something you've written that's at least 2500 words long. That's about 8-9 pages of single-spaced text (more or less.)

The minimum for publishing on Amazon KDP is 2500 words. So that's your target.

A Cover

This is simply two things: Big Text and Big Image.

Hold your thumb up at arms length. You should be able to read and understand the cover on your thumb at that size. That's why they call those images "thumbnails." When they shrink down to that size it still should be readable. Go on Amazon and look up some books and see what is "also recommended" lower on the page.

See what you find there? Small covers you can still read and understand.

The simplest approach to make covers is to use **Canva.com** online – they've got a lot of book cover templates there, designed specifically for Amazon KDP. Download the finished product to your computer.

Or you could use any of the other free online book cover creators out there as well.

Description

When you get to this point, just type in a sentence that describes your book. As much or as little as you want.

Why this simple?

Because once you've done these steps, you'll have your first book up there and you'll only get better from here on out.

One study says that most people (about 80%) have a book they want to write. But only about 10% ever do write it. And only about 10% of them actually get it published.

The whole point of this lesson is to simply get you over this learning curve of publishing your own book.

Look, if you don't like any part of it, Amazon and all ebook outlets will let you change what you put up there. At any time you want, today, tomorrow, or years from now.

The key point is to do it *now* and get it _done_.

Yes, it's that simple.

And just that free.

In just a half an hour, you proved to yourself that you can publish any time you feel like it.

Yes, the next books you write and publish will be better.

You just accomplished more than most. You're now in that elite group called published authors. Time to update your business card and online profiles.

So, take a break, go get your favorite beverage and celebrate!

2. Get Your Basics In

– blog, email provider, publishing accounts, uber-reader social media. (Advanced: IFTTT)

First, Get Set Up for Business

You're going to have to have four points covered to succeed:

1. A Blog. This is not always used, but you'll find that it will enable you to communicate to your audience and give you a place where you can post your stories. This is a central place where people can find more about you. They can comment on your books and then you can reply to them. Blogger is recommended as you don't have to worry about maintaining the backend. It's always been secure. Pick out a look and feel you like and get started. There are many good references on how to set up a blog. I'll have write-ups in the membership when you join.

2. An Email Provider. This is an email service. The secret to the successful writers is that they all have an email list that their readers go onto. In this way, they have a personal line to communicate with readers and tell them when new releases are coming out, special offers, and so on. MailChimp is one of the most recommended, since it's free to start with, but there are many.

3. Publishing accounts. These are KDP (which you already have) and also ebook aggregators that post your books for you: Smashwords, Direct2Digital, StreetLib, and PublishDrive. Those will get you pretty much to every major and minor ebook outlet these days. Print: Lulu.com Hands down the simplest and most reliable print-on-demand service in the business. It doesn't cost you anything to put a book up there or do your revisions. You will have to buy a copy as proof, but you'll want one anyway. They distribute to Amazon and Ingrams directly. And consider Findaway for audiobooks. [Still researching this...] Get your accounts set up now. Now.

4. While you already have some social media accounts, the only three you need to actively work at are **Wattpad, Goodreads, and Library Thing.** The short answer to your question: because this is where the uber-readers go to find more books to read. Uber-readers drive the ebook market. They are known to read as many as two full-length novels a day, while the average reader finishes 12 books a year. All of these sites will build audiences, and enable you to find other authors to network with. LibraryThing may also help you get your books in to libraries, which is another route uber-readers use to find books.

Second, Read and Write Daily

Two habits you have to develop as an author in order to succeed come from studying successful authors and what their recommendations are over and over and over. You'll find successful authors recommend and are caught doing these two things daily.

1. They read daily, and
2. They write daily.

You have to get into reading other people's works, the works that you like, that you most enjoy. This also counts for non-fiction. You read what you most like and you study it. If you like to read it, then you'll like to write it.

The additional part of this is to write every day. You need to write every day. Writers write. You read every day and you write every day. Through that you absorb other successful writer's plots, characters, sentence choice, descriptions, summaries, backgrounds, worldviews, etc. So you're constantly have this flowing in your system like oxygen and blood.

I've seen authors that appear to suddenly come out of nowhere and within several months they're actually having bestseller books up there, good selling books. You check just prior to that to find what they were doing. One author was watching movies as a film critic for a living. Another said he was a that he was an avid reader and he would just go through books like a hot knife through butter. You check these back and all of them have a love of books and read constantly, and they will write constantly. Of course there's exceptions this, but I'm telling you what I found for the vast majority of them. Chase them back and you'll find they love to read and then they learned how to love to write. You really have to enjoy what you're doing every day.

3. Learning to Write What You Love to Read.

– Get the PD and bestsellers in the genre you like to read the most. Finalize with Steve Scott approach

Listening to podcasts and videos recently, a single question was mentioned by a couple of productive authors in two completely different areas.

They asked: why are you writing something you aren't liking?

If you don't like it, your audience isn't going to like it.

And their whole point is that you should read what you like and write what you like and enjoy your life thoroughly.

That is the whole basis behind working as an author and making a living at it, or even if you make a living at something else. Why are you doing something if you don't like doing it?

The trick to finding what to write is very close to that. You pick your genres/categories based on two points:

1. Do you love reading these types of books?

2. Are their people buying these books – enough to make a living at it?

What you don't want to do is to start writing in some area because it "makes a lot of money for other authors." That's the world's worst reason. You won't write your best material, and so your readers won't buy it after they sample it.

Writers are there to package experiences and transport readers to different worlds. Readers want to be transported, they expect it. Anything you do that throws them out of their reading makes them want to quit reading that book. And not buy any more like it.

Just because you like reading in some genres doesn't mean you should write in them. There are a lot of people writing and making good income from Romance. The trick to that is that there is so much demand and so much supply that the entire area is very price sensitive. The trick is that they expect you to price your books below $3.00 and you'll have to compete against over 40,000 other books in some of these sub-genres. The genre of Westerns is also popular, and profitable. However the average price is below $2.00

To figure out where you can publish on your own without advanced analytics, you're looking to write and publish in areas that have very low competition. Yet there aren't enough books being published, according to the buyers. Profitable income is supplying demand where there is not enough supply. Always has been that way, always will be.

There are some exceptions to any rule, including this one. But you won't know until you research for yourself.

The way Steve Scott and others tell you to find a category is to select a one and look at the sales of the top few and bottom few of the top twenty. The first few should be under 20K in their sales rank. The bottom few should be greater than 50K in sales rank. This means that with a little work, you can wind up on the front page and move up to become a "bestseller" in that category. Meanwhile, people are buying enough of your books to make it profitable.

Dave Chessom of Kindlepreneur has a different (more severe) take:

- It should have fewer than 4 ebooks with an Amazon Best Seller Rank (ABSR) less than of <10,000
- It should have fewer than 7 ebooks with the keyword in their title and or subtitle
- It should have fewer than 2 with Best Seller marks
- At least 2 ebooks should have an ABSR less than 100,000 – shows there are decent sales

That means you look up the areas you most like to read (make a list to start with, probably) and then run them though the steps above. It may take you all of an afternoon, or maybe a day or two. But it's research well worth it.

When you do narrow it down, then be sure to check out what the covers look like, what keywords they are using in their descriptions. You can also purchase individual studies from k-lytics just on the genres you are most interested in. His videos and PDF's are very revealing, and are a good investment.

If you write what you love to read, and can earn a livable income doing it, then you're well on your way.

4. Start Dissecting Plots

– per the Story Circle and 7-Points System (or anything else you want to use. Read, Study, Dissect, Plot.

Dan Wells used to have a series of videos up on YouTube where he talks about plots and story arcs. He said honestly that he got it from the Star Trek RPG Narrator's Guide. You can find that book on Scribd.com as a PDF. Somebody scanned pages wholesale, so it's a 150 Meg download.

It starts about page 51, and explains the 7 points that are needed to write a story.

Your ask the what-if question. That assumes a protagonist and it assumes an antagonist or the villain. There is always a conflict of some type.

From there the RPG Narrator's Guide says to go to the end and lay out the outcome of this whole thing. Then you go to the beginning and your hero will be in the opposite situation. Dan Wells, on his video, used Harry Potter as an example: he winds up as a boy wizard at the end, but he starts off living under the stairs in some Muggle's home, about as low as you can get.

So you have your ending and have your beginning. Then you go to the middle and ask yourself, "What's the change that has to happen?" The change is usually where the hero gets enough trials and lessons to become proactive. He's gotten enough solutions and resources where he can start taking the chase to the villain instead of being chased by the villain the whole time.

Now between the beginning and the middle is a plot turn. And this plot turn is where they decide to take the challenge, they decide to go on the journey.

The second plot turn is halfway between the midpoint and the end, or somewhere in there, where the hero is really in a very bad situation, around where your final confrontation happens and he beats the living snot out of the villain (as opposed to the villain beating the snot out of him, as he has been for the rest of the story to this point.)

In between the midpoint and the two plot turns are pinch points. These points are where concentrated effort happens in order to move the plot forward. These usually involve a lot of the characters all going into the same location in one episode and all reacting as some sort of action. The result usually puts the protagonist into another bad situation, but it moves the plot forward.

Because the general theory to the three-act structure is Start-Middle-End. The second act is twice as long as other two parts, so it can really be split in two and then you have your Four Act structure.

And that's what you see on TV in between the commercials.

A guy who's worked out the basics this is Dan Harmon and his Story Circle.

The 7-point system aligns to the Story Circle, which aligns to the Hero's Journey, and aligns to Save The Cat beat system, and so on.

They all follow the same cycles. The Story Circle is one which starts making sense out of everything. In all my research, I haven't seen any description of how to plot which doesn't follow the same basic storyline, just different in their ways of doing it. Find the one which works best for you, then use it.

Another effective way is to actually watch movies, especially TV shows. Geoff Shaw recommends this and has a nice course on Udemy about it. I recommend you get DVD sets where the series has been on TV for several years and kept going and going and going. This will give you the longer story arcs which hold the whole story together.

And that's what you're ideally writing. Because writing in series and serials is the way you can enable your readers to find your other works and stay tuned into them.

You can take apart these stories and split them into their four parts. Put them into their Story Cycle and work out all the characters in them. Grid these out and take notes. Then you'll have a working story that you can then rework and use as a base to develop your own story with different characters, different settings, and so on. You don't just copy. You recombine and reinvent the plot enough to keep it interesting. Romeo and Juliet has been redone dozens of times. The most successful was West Side Story. The main thing is to start studying these shows as stories. Learn to expect what's going to happen because you know where the story is going to go. You know where the plot turns have to be, and all the parts.

Now you can write all the fiction stories you want.

5. Learn To Speak Your Book To Life

– Transcribe with GoogleChrome/Docs, Dragon Naturally Speaking, or Trint.com (or enhanced dictation on the MAC.) Keep these simple. Upload your results to Wattpad for crowd-editing/review.

People can talk faster than they can type. (In general. We'll leave the typing speed-champions out of this.) The average speaker talks about 150 words per minute. On the news, they can get up to 250 words or faster if they need to. A person can speak around 9K - 12K words in an hour. But the average writer will fall between five hundred and a thousand words an hour. A fast writer will do about 5K words an hour. So at top speed, you can talk at least twice as fast as you can type.

The trick, then, is getting it transcribed. There are programs for this, such as Dragon Naturally Speaking, which is a bit of an investment and learning curve. There is another online service, called Trint.com, which will allow you to upload a recording and then edit it directly while you listen to it, and will cost you about 25 cents a minute. You can then download the final text. Other services will transcribe for you for about $1 a minute, which is the average rate. If you want higher accuracy or faster turnaround, it will cost you more. But you'll still have to edit the work once you get it back, regardless.

If you have a MAC, you can download their enhanced dictation, which is pretty good. Google also helped us out by incorporating this into their Chrome browser on their Google Docs. Most of this book was originally transcribed that way. It does need an active Internet access, fairly fast. The trick with Google Docs is that you actually have to watch the screen because it will quit on you if you get involved in telling the story and then not transcribe what you're saying.

But with practice, you can keep an eye on it to make sure it's working. Obviously, this takes some getting used to, if you type everything. My limited testing shows that this does change your writing style, but it's far more normal to talk a story than it is to wrestle is around in your mind and then manually type it out.

If you figure that you can spend 2 hours a day speaking your book, four days a week, then you'll be able to have about 80K words by the end of a week. Then you can start editing them into shape. If you're writing only 500 words a day, it's going to take you about three months to get to that point. 5K words per day will take you 16 days, and so on.

You can see how this is more efficient. Spend the second week editing it or however it works for you. Shorter works are simpler to edit, so you might want to edit the short works as you get them done that day.

You've also seen how talking your book can at least double your writing speed. It takes some getting used to. People who have experience in drama and public speaking will have an easier time of it – or not.

The Secret to Learning To Talk Stories.

Read out loud.

Yes, that's the trick. Find short stories in the area you want to write in. Read these out loud to yourself each night (or to your children.) This is one of the ways of learning, much like copywriters would take other's ads and hand write them in order to internalize the patterns they used in those ads.

Get collections of short stories in your genre and read them out loud every night. Then go through and dissect them according to the Story Circle for the plot elements and how they were used. Download the most popular short stories on Gutenberg. Then fill up a notebook by dissecting each story.

You can outline a story based on that plot dissection and speak it out.

Another thing to do is to record your thoughts as a journal. Get used to forming sentences without pauses, stutters, hesitations, etc.

I recorded an idea I had while checking my cattle on their pasture, and that 18 minutes of talking wound up with 1800 words of usable text.

Speaking your book affects your ability to publish by speeding up it radically.

6. Learn The Four Steps Of Writing Great Books Fast

– sentence, paragraph, page, cover. Hook, premise, synopsis. Leverage everything.

Now here's how you start a book (of course, test this out for yourself):

Before you write anything, before you even work out the plot, you come up with a "what if" statement. Like what if I was visiting a hotel in the middle of nowhere, going to a conference, and open the bathroom up to find my best friend murdered in there. Just then I hear a knock at the door and it's the police and I've been framed. I heard this over the radio where a guy thought this up in his hotel room attending a conference. This is the whole point. You're constantly looking around the world that you live in as a big plot inspiration.

Everything around you will give you a "what if?" if you're looking for it. You see a wild bird: What if I could talk to wild animals and what would they tell me? You can go humorous with this. Imagine the unexpected to find something that's funny. I thought it was pretty funny a few years ago that somebody was blaming cow farts as one of the causes of global warming. A plot could be made out of that as a conspiracy to feed dairy cattle a certain flatulent ingredient in order to raise local temperatures and affect weather, and so cover up a crime. (And efforts by politicians and lawyers to fix it just made it worse – all that hot air...) Fantastic idea, but that's all fiction is - making the dull and humdrum world we live in become more interesting.

There are four things you need before you start writing a book.

First is your what-if and then that becomes a sentence.

Second is to write a paragraph. It's more like your elevator speech. 35 seconds to describe your book or pitch it to a media producer. That's the time it takes you to go between one floor to the next. The doors close. Someone asks you what your book's about. You'd say, "Well it's Alien meets Gulliver on the desert island of Robinson Crusoe." Some say this is how film concepts are pitched. Like "Gidget goes to Hogwarts". Go a little further than that and you have your main characters in there and the plot and everything. You have a couple sentences in a paragraph that actually explain the entire story. It doesn't explain everything and leads the media guy to get off with you to find out more. This is also how you pitch a story to the media. You have about that much time to get it across. They are very busy people and that is their alloted attention span to your new idea.

The third part is to write a whole page on your book idea. That page is also what they call a one-sheet, what the book distributors want from you, so they can sell your idea to their book stores to get them to carry your book.

The three parts again are to write a sentence, a paragraph, and a page. A what-if hook, a 35-second elevator speech, and a page of data that becomes your description.

The fourth part is getting a cover made. I've recently seen a video where Chris Fox commissions all the covers for his books before he really starts writing anything.

When you get the cover made, you can print it out and hang it up where you can see it. You are keeping the end in mind constantly. You can do this yourself. Print it out so you can wrap it around another book you have. You can stand it up against your computer monitor for more inspiration.

If You Can Measure It, You Can Improve It.

This is a core datum for any production. We don't have to go overboard with this, but the general idea is that you want to improve your production volume by improving efficiency. While I strongly recommend learning to speak your books, if you're more comfortable typing, then keep doing what works for you.

You'll want to set up a spreadsheet or even a ruled paper taped or pinned to a board in your workspace. Note down date, words produced, words edited (usable text you wound up with.) Chris Fox sets daily targets. He then knows where he will need to get to, by when, in order to have his book ready on time.

You may want to also note down where you produced it and what you were doing then.

7. The Second Big Lie: Building Your "Platform"

– Vision, Content, Audience, Network. Get TGR by Nap Hill and do those 6 steps. You already have a system in place to write and publish your books. By posting to Wattpad, you build your audience. By interacting on Goodreads, you'll find other authors to network with. If you can, get into Nick Stephenson's [Authors Network] And start getting interviews on podcast and radio shows. Try contacting shows on iTunes New and Notable, or simply pay a nominal fee to [Radio Interviews] And there's far more material in the full book.

- - - -

The Second Lie Authors Are Fed: You Have To Build a "Platform" To Be Successful.

The biggest problem with authorities is they all define different things when they talk about "platform." They define it in their terms of what they ran into when they were trying to get started as an author. Most of them say a platform is social media. And that's a bunch of bull.

Most of them say it's the network you have. A lot of them say it's "influencers." But while they all talk about it, they don't know they are all describing the same four pieces that make up a platform, even without pointing them out.

The problem is that they're not telling you all the pieces. They are just telling the pieces they know of.

Here's the four pieces:

The First Is Your Vision.

This is exactly what you consider it can be. It's what you want to accomplish as an author. It's the end-goal in your mind.

Second Is Your Content.

That's the books you write, and all the text you write, but it's also all the ads and any descriptions you write about your books. It's also anywhere you write or talk about your book or the experiences it contains, anywhere at all. That's your content you've produced.

The Third Point Is Your Audience.

Who will listen to you when you talk about something? This is where a lot of authors struggle at their beginning. Nobody has ever heard of them. These authors don't know wants to listen. You can't just get off a bus in the middle of New York City, talk about your book, and expect anybody to listen. You need to find places where readers gather. Then find readers for that story type.

The Fourth Part Is Your Network.

These are all the people you do business with. And they're all the people that have audiences from front of them like media hosts, podcast, and radio hosts. They're also other authors that have similar readers to yours. If you were running a regular business you'd have plumbers, electricians, building and repairing your shop. You would have your regular customers that come in. And the business owners on your street would be in your network. It's where you buy the gas for your car from. In a small town, everybody knows everybody, and everybody is in their other network and also in everybody else's network.

So when you come out with a book and you tell them, they tell their friends and other relatives they know and that's where you will get your book sales. Most authors get their get their first sales that way. That is also the end of their book sales. Because that is all the network they've developed.

How the System Works

We want to build up an audience through readers who want to read your book. We want to build up a network of people who want to share your book to their audiences, so your audience grows. We want to build your vision: What you want to accomplish. Where you want to end. That vision says how much money you want to make, how much income you want to produce. It's how much effect you want to create with this book.

All those will determine what content you want to/need to write. They predict your needed investment to get that result.

The trick with these four points is that they are a natural system, everybody has this. Learning to walk and then to run. "Practice Makes Permanent." All the elements in this system are interactive. So when you improve one you improve all of them. And if you screw up one you'll bring the others down. But that's very unlikely. Because if you get your vision straight about what you want to accomplish, and if you make this your burning desire (as Napoleon Hill described it.) You get everything else off your plate, or just let those distractions slide away, so you can just concentrate on that one goal in front of you. Then you'll be able to succeed and grow and expand your writing to whatever you need to.

Your vision will also encompass how much of a network you want, how much of an audience you need, and how much and what type of content you need to produce. It will also tell you how much you need to work on improving your vision.

As you publish, your network will then tell you whether that was a hit or a failure with their audience. Inappropriate content. So change it next time. Study them. Learn what they want. Deliver what they expect. Just as you do in your writing.

And your audience will either react or they won't. But the point is you need a big enough and vocal audience to give you the feedback necessary to revise your content. If it's your network's audience, you want to work to please those audiences so you please network people. Those sales will or won't give you enough income to satisfy your vision. Your main effort in this might be to see how much audience you can add. See how these four points fit together?

8. What We've Learned.

The whole point of this was to show you how simple and easy it is to get your book out.

You won't have to be nagged by your muse anymore. You now have a way to get those inspired story ideas up and out of your head into a recording and into print.

I created this course for you to get you started. Because I saw all this money being spent on courses and books and everything that just make it even harder to get started.

If you can tell a story that people like to hear, you can publish a book.

It's really that simple. If it takes you a half hour to record it, another hour to edit it, another 15 minutes to make a cover, 5 minutes to get it up on Amazon, then you can publish a book in an hour and 20 minutes.

There's no reason not to do it today. Starting now.

And the books you publish will just keep getting better as you go.

Let's recap what you've learned:

1. All you need to get published is 2500 words of text, a sentence of description, and a cover. And you don't have to pay anyone for any of these. It will take you maybe a half-hour to get everything up there, depending on how long it takes to find or combine something you wrote to that length.

2. Set up your writing business to be a business. Blog, Email, Publishing Accounts, Social Media accounts on Goodreads, LibraryThing, Wattpad. And you still didn't have to spend anything except your time to get these. Not one red cent. Then get your two basic habits in: Write Daily, Read Daily.

3. Write what you love to read and people will pay you for. This takes some research, but again, you can do this for just the time it takes. Maybe a day or two, but then you'll know.

4. Start dissecting those stories you read and the TV shows you watch. Study plotting and pick out a simple method you can follow that will make sense of the stories you read and watch. Then get the into the habit of dissecting everything, so you can get even more ideas to write and publish.

5. Start speaking your book if you can. This will double or quadruple your word production daily. You'll have to work out a way to get transcripts. Sure, otherwise just type. But make sure you write daily, regardless.

6. Lay out your book's four first steps before you even outline the plot: A sentence. A paragraph. A page. And the cover, an inspiration to keep you going. Only then do you take those parts and build a full outline of it and begin talking or typing your book out.

Those six steps above will get you going right now, today.

If you haven't started already, then put this book down or pause the recording and do it now.

Best of luck to all of us.

PS. Email me your results. I'd love to hear them.

Bonus Lesson: The 10,000 Foot Look At Author Freedom

Overview:

Starting from nothing means you use content to build your audience and network. Your vision is first, of course. That is the only limiting factor to your success. This is a content-oriented approach. And according to research is the one that always works.

Your main point is to quickly get a deep backbench of material up there so that readers who like your work can find other books by that author or in that series.

What you don't want to do is worry about promoting and "making money" right off. These will come in due time. All the current 6- and 7-figure authors started out years earlier by producing substantial amounts of content. Even J. K. Rowling didn't really start rollling in the income until her fifth book was published. The single-book successes were posting their work on blogs and in forums years before they first published anything. They built their audience with content, massive amounts of content.

The trick is that it doesn't have to take years. It does take a lot of work. And the faster you can produce quality works that engage the reader with great experiences, the faster your income will rise.

This course is to set you one the path to learning your basics. Once you have your production basics in place and can crank out good content without killing yourself from over-work, then you can expand into building your platform and promoting in order to increase your income.

But in every—single—case: it's great amounts of great content first.

Rules:

Always:

publish short,

publish in series,

publish by pen name,

publish in as many formats as possible.

Publish collections for the longer readers, but never the entire series in one book. Collections should have additional material in them that the single books don't, such as Part 2 having the first story in the next series.

Co-author your pen names as you can. Publish collections of all the first books in your series when you have several out there.

First book in series is always permafree, second is an opt-in bonus (but also on sale) third and rest (8 is recommended) are at regular pricing.

Regular pricing is .99 for first month and then raise to $2.99 and price according to length after that.

Note: some genres (you shouldn't be writing in if you want serious income) are price sensitive, such as Romance, Westerns.

Write faster than you can publish.

What you track, you can improve. Keep spreadsheets of words produced, word edited, books published, etc. Sales have their own metrics. Your concentration to begin with is on producing as much great books as you can, as quickly as you can. You need to get ahead of the feeding times.

Suggestions:

Create pen names in related sub-genres so that moving to a nearby genre isn't as hard as a completely different one. Cosy Mysteries and Women Sleuths are very similar, compared to Military Science Fiction. And it's likely those two authors would co-write as they have similar interests.

This will speed mastering the different genres.

Two pen names can write four series A, B, A-B, B-A. Four pen names give 12 possible co-author combinations.

Appendix

Online course and additional materials are available at

http://livesensical.com/go/author-freedom/

Bibliography

"Becoming a Writer" by Dorothea Brande
https://goo.gl/gpVap0

"Wake Up and Live" by Dorothea Brande
https://goo.gl/TyZ0hJ

"On Writing" by Stephen King
http://amzn.com/B000FC0SIM/

"Elements of Style" by William Strunk Jr. and E.B. White
http://amzn.com/0205313426/

"Building Your Book for Kindle" by Kindle Direct
Publishing http://amzn.com/B007URVZJ6/

"Lulu Content Creation Guide" by Lulu Press Inc.
https://goo.gl/GjkNZ

"Smashwords Style Guide" by Mark Coker
http://www.smashwords.com/books/view/52

"An Open Office Guide to Publishing on Smashwords"
by Gregory Scott
http://www.smashwords.com/books/view/252868

"Secrets to Ebook Publishing Success" by Mark Coker
http://www.smashwords.com/books/view/145431

"Content, Inc." by Joe Pulizzi
http://amzon.com/B0141KT528

"From 2,000 to 5,000" by Rachel Aaron
(http://amzn.com/B009NKXAWS)

"Story Grid" by Shawn Coyne
(http://amzn.com/B00WT7TP8A)

"Reader Magnets" by Nick Stephenson
(http://amzn.com/B00PCKIJ4C)

Other books in this series

Visit http://livesensical.com/book-series/publishing-and-writing/
Available on Amazon, Lulu, and as Pay What You Want

Really Simple Writing & Publishing
Learn How to Write, Design, Format, Upload, and Sell Your Own Book for Low Cost or Free. (http://livesensical.com/book/really-simple-writing-publishing/)

J'APE: Just Another Publicity Excuse
How to Publish Your (Kindle) Book for Shameless Self-Promotion and Profit (http://livesensical.com/book/jape-just-another-publicity-excuse-parody-celebrity-self-publishing/)

Publish. Profit. Independence.
How to Earn Extra Income and Financial Freedom by Publishing on Your Own (http://livesensical.com/book/publish-profit-independence/)

How to Write Less and Profit More
A Rich Adventure in Short Read Kindle Publishing (http://livesensical.com/book/write-less-profit-rich-adventure-short-read-kindle-publishing/)

Writing Serial Fiction in the Real World
A Simple, Tongue-in-Cheek Guide to Writing and Publishing Episodic eBooks for Profit on Amazon (and Elsewhere.) (http://livesensical.com/book/writing-serial-fiction-real-world/)

How to Help Librarians Fall in Love With Your Self-Published Book
...and Get More Sales When They Do. (http://livesensical.com/book/help-librarians-love-book/)

Cracking the Kindle Sales Code
How to Search Engine Optimize Your Titles and Descriptions so Amazon Promotes Your Book and Recommends Buyers to You at No Cost (http://livesensical.com/book/cracking-kindle-sales-code/)

Your Kindle Booksales Blueprint
How to Break Out of the No-Sales Amazon Self-Publishing Basement and Routinely Start Getting Regular Passive Income From Your Kindle Booksales Without Added Expense or Tricks (http://livesensical.com/book/kindle-booksales-blueprint/)

Related Writing Texts Published by Midwest Journal Press

See: http://livesensical.com/go/writing-refs/

Carolyn Wells' Mystery Story Technique for Writers
Creating Your Children's Book by Thrive Learning Institute Library

Technique of Fiction Writing by Robert Saunders Dowst
Becoming the Fiction Storyteller of Your Dreams by Robert C. Worstell, Dorothea Brande, and Marie Shedlock

Additional References:

Formatting guides:
Amazon (http://amzn.com/B007URVZJ6)

Lulu.com (http://connect.lulu.com/t5/eBook-Formatting-Publishing/eBook-Creator-Guide/ta-p/109443)

Smashwords (http://www.smashwords.com/books/view/52)

Cover sizes article - Mark Coker, Smashwords (https://goo.gl/ECEWV)

Amazon re: cover sizes (https://goo.gl/S3S0op)

Key tip:

"Regardless of how they appear on the cover, title and subtitle must be correctly capitalized. The first letter of all words in the title and subtitle should be capitalized, except for the following words: a, an, and, for, from, of, or, the, to. The first and last word of the title and subtitle should always be capitalized."

Video: How to publish a book on Linux or Windows – at no cost - https://youtu.be/90wJf1pmi-8

Get Scam Free

Visit this page for free education on scammers and how to handle them: http://livesensical.com/scamfree/ (No opt-in required.)

Free tools

These three are all I use to publish my books. They run on every commonly-known platform.

- **LibreOffice** (a version of Openoffice) - reads and can save as Word documents.
  (http://www.libreoffice.org/download/)
- **Calibre** – builds a library for your ebooks and holds metadata (http://calibre-ebook.com/download)
- **GIMP** – to make covers.
  (http://www.gimp.org/downloads/)

Recording and editing your own audio (for books, etc.)

- **Audacity** (http://www.audacityteam.org/download/)

Paid Tools

BetterBookTools.com - to make finding profitable categories simpler and faster. Also has a built-in editor for your descriptions (among other things.) http://www.betterbooktools.com/

KDPRocket – to help you find the best choice of keywords in your chosen genre (among other things.) https://kdprocket.com/

KindleSpy – a nice in-browser tool to help you see exactly what the competition is doing and download spreadsheet-ready data (among other things.) http://www.kdspy.com/

Recommended Courses

Kindling by Geoff Shaw.
http://www.5minutepublishing.com/kindling/ Use "kdspy" as discount code

Nick Stephenson's Your First 10000 Readers -
http://www.yourfirst10kreaders.com/

Mark Dawson's Facebook Advertising Course -
http://www.selfpublishingformula.com/

Related Sites:

Kindlepreneur.com by Dave Chessom (http://kindlepreneur.com/)

Author Marketing Club by Jim Kukral
(http://authormarketingclub.com/members/about/)

Special Supplements

I've pulled some short pieces from an earlier book in this series to help you where you are now. A warning: these contradict the "best authorities" and what passes for "conventional wisdom." So be prepared to have people say you're wrong if you try them and they work.

Lesson 1 Supplement - Your Author Why Brings Success

There is a reason you do things. There is a reason your books succeed or fail.

It's your Why.

Simon Sinek wrote a very good book for managers called "Start With Why." It has everything to do with your author success.

This really starts with your Vision part of your Platform.

The bulk of this book is about the How's you use to create the effect you've always wanted.

But its the Why which you should always value above everything else. This is what motivates you and it will motivate your readers.

I was on a group page for authors yesterday, updating myself on what the current strategies are and what's working. The striking point was that the authors who were making it big had big dreams.

Their vision was their story. You could say that they were traveling their life path to find how it would turn out.

But more than that, this also had to do with the quality of their writing. Another success story there was accompanied by a commentary from another author. She stated that his success was from three years of hard work, writing to market they knew was profitable and producing just what that market wanted.

This is the value of your Content again, adding into your vision. You also see the Audience there. Just going to that group page was being part of that Network.

Underlying your platform, is your Why. What's your story? What is it that gets you up with fresh inspiration in the morning?

There was another entry by a writer who wanted suggestions about how she could keep track of all the story ideas that would come to her "out of the blue" and she wanted to keep track of them. (I suggested a smartphone recording, or even text herself. Just stand still while you are doing this – be safe.)

The point of her problem was that she was learning to live "in the Zone" as a writer, despite still having a day job. She was on her way to success, as long as she kept her feet directly on that story-path she was following with her life.

All the courses and books I've read mention this to a greater or lesser degree. Jeff Goins' books deal almost exclusively with this area.

You just have to make it part of your regular activities. Look over the four parts of your platform during your "business time" and make a to-do list of what you need to improve each one. For Vision, it's can be just a certain amount of time to meditate and improve your vision.

- Using J. B. Jones' notebook method of reviewing what you want to have and be daily is another.

- Claude M. Bristol had you writing short phrases on the back of business cards and sticking these on your desk, and any personal mirror you saw every day, to remind you of your goals.

- Napoleon Hill and Earl Nightingale suggested you write your goal out in a few sentences on the back of an index card you could carry with you. Then review that first thing in the morning, during your lunch hour, last thing at night.

- Hill later recommended doing this 12 times a day. In all these cases, you concentrate or focus on getting the positive feelings which are present when you achieve, acquired, or attained that (note the past tense, there) that goal.

It was my observation that the authors who were telling about how they've been doing this for years with no result weren't following what I've said above.

Their posts were negative, and this was probably their consistent view of their own life.

Hill mentioned you should "burn your bridges" in pursuing your "burning desire." I've seen this with successful authors such as Chris Fox. He started off his video channel with a 21 day challenge of writing and publishing a book. Every day for 21 days he recorded what he had done. So he had accountability built in. And that book is still one of his better-selling books.

The point is to find and follow your Bliss. Dive into your own adventure. Live life fully.

Income finds success. Be successful by setting and achieving your writing goals and then your income will follow.

It's just that simple.

From Desire to Reality in Six Easy Steps

(from *How to Completely Change Your Life in 30 Seconds, Part I* by Earl Nightingale)

Six definite practical steps to transform a burning desire into reality.

1. Fix in your mind an exact picture of what you desire. It's not sufficient merely to say, for example, "I want plenty of money." Be definite as to the amount.

2. Determine exactly what you intend to give in return for the thing you desire. There's no such reality as something for nothing.

3. Establish a definite date by which you intend to possess the desired thing.

4. Create a definite plan for carrying out your desire and begin at once, whether you feel entirely ready or not to put this plan into action.

5. Write out a clear, concise statement of your responses to the preceding four steps.

6. Read your written statement aloud twice daily. Once after arising in the morning and once just before retiring at night. As you read, see and feel and believe yourself already in possession of whatever your goal happens to be.

"Through some strange and powerful principle of mental chemistry, nature wraps up in the impulse [of a] strong desire that something which recognizes no such word as impossible and accepts no such reality as failure." - Napoleon Hill

Lesson 2 Supplement - Your Lever to Move the World

The great mathematician and philosopher Archimedes once stated "give me a lever, a place to stand, and I will move the world."

This says everything about an author's platform. Given a place to hang their hat, any author is able to build both audience and network from there, then leverage these with content according to your vision.

1. A Blog

Geoff Shaw, in his Kindling Course, recommends an author have a blog so they can communicate with their audience. He gives the example of J. A. Konrath who has only ever had a Blogger blog to fill that function. (http://jakonrath.blogspot.com/)

With RSS feeds, a fan can keep up with all your updates, independently of any emails you'd send out to announce things. As well, Google will send you traffic to a greater or lesser degree, depending on what you are writing about and how much competition is writing about similar things.

If you are writing about your successful books, then it's likely people who are looking for those will see Amazon and your links, as well as the other places your books show up.

2. An Email Service

Again, this is a way to keep in touch with your fans. You can send out broadcasts to all your list, or subdivide them into those who more regularly open your emails, what their preferences are, etc.

An email service also enables you to build up your beta readers, who can help you proof your books and give you a lineup of reviews right out of the starting gate.

At this writing, probably the best starter service is MailChimp. It integrates with services like Instafreebie to build your list, and is free up to 2,000 subscribers. While you have to pay for additional services like being able to send out pre-scheduled emails (called an auto-responder series) those costs are quite low overall.

The competition among email service providers is fierce, such that they keep up with their peers and provide mostly the same options within a month or two of a competitor rolling out theirs.

3. Course/Membership

This just brings your fans even closer. Both of these are usually on an opt-in basis, so you have their emails. They can be free or paid. In both cases, they offer more services and access to the author. And you can then offer them more free and paid services that they would appreciate.

Fiction writers usually have memberships, as is promoted in this book. But I've seen many of them (Dawson and Stephenson) giving back to the community by sharing what they know – and getting paid for it – by using courses.

Tim Grahl pointed out the financial leverage of having a course. He wrote a non-fiction book, "Your First 1000 Copies" and pushed it to get 10,000 copies sold in the first year, advertising and appearing on podcasts.

The book itself netted him $16K. His business, which is launching books, basically, netted an additional $50K in services bought. But when he made a course based on that book, he pulled in an additional $150K...

No kidding.

That's real leverage.

4. The Book As an Experience Container

Your book has ideas in it, it has experiences in it. Your book doesn't have to be in any set format. Let's list the common ones:

- ebook
- paperback
- hardback
- audiobook
- course
- video
- podcast
- CD
- DVD
- Movie

- and foreign translations of these as well.

The common reason for any success with these is the experience you provide. It is a good enough or insufficient experience that they tell others about this, sharing it. And so the common mantra that the first thing an author should do is "Write A Damn Good Book."

Your production line can start with any of these products and create the rest based on that content. If you start out with text, you can record it for audio, match that up with a presentation and have video.

What that enables is for anyone to get the version they most prefer to experience.

Again, leverage.

Find you your own place to stand, use the leverage of your choice, and move your world to where you want it.

Lesson 3 Supplement - Writing and Mastering One Genre First

Very, very needful. Most writers never get out of a single genre and make their income just from writing several series there. (Chris Fox writes in Military Science Fiction and found that writing in Trilogies is most profitable.)

To test the above workflow, write a series of 8 short stories that build your world with background episodes. These may or may not wind up in the book. Those don't matter as much as getting the workflow down while you write entertaining stories.

You are looking for completed story circles in each short story, and also including the various expected conventions and obligatory scenes.

If you don't feel comfortable by the end of these, then write eight more. Take the first ones down and publish them if they are any good. You are publishing under a pen name, and not linking that pen name to your author page. If they fail, it's a good test. You can always take them down and replace them with a new set. You also want to check how they do as both short reads/short stories and as a collection. Don't worry about reviews. Price them at .99 to get some early traction.

Again, to be efficient, keep all your stories in the world you are building. Once you feel confident about your skills, then plot out a longer story and all it's episodes. This may be by first writing a four-part short story to get used to getting the Story Circle plot understood and applied.

Then maybe write a two-parter, where part one is in four chapters, and part two is the concluding four chapters.

Then a four-part series, then you'll be ready for an eight-part series.

Once you can execute an eight-part series, then you'll be ready to improve your efficiency to get this all done in one week.

You may want to do several of these eight-part series, so you can get used to producing them week after week.

Lesson 4 Supplement - How to Tear Down a Perfectly Good Story

Read, Study, Plot, Write.

Read (or watch) the story straight through.

Read or watch it your story the first time for enjoyment.

Grab your folded tabloid sheet (use a clipboard to make it manageable on your lap) and quickly write down the points which stand out in our head. Also note down any story ideas which have come to you as you're watching. (Pause the video if you are watching, as you won't remember them later.)

Re-read the story and dissect it.

Divide your sheet with lines into four parts, either stacked vertically, or in quarters, like the Story Circle

Note the 7 points. Find the plot-turn points and the pinch points, as well as the beginning and end. Write down a one sentence summary of the story at that those points. Write down the hook and teaser summaries as well.

Now fill in the characters, what changes they made, what reaction points, what try/fail actions they took. Any aha moments. Plot the whole thing out. (Again, if you come up with a story idea, note it down somewhere that's not part of the plot sheet itself.)

You may want to read or watch it one more time to make sure you've got all the details straight. This time you can look for nuances in dialog, and character treatments.

Write Your Own New, Improved Version

Now take that plot and write your own story from it, with a sentence, paragraph, page approach:

- Sentence is the hook. Should be within 140 characters so you can tweet it.
- Paragraph is the elevator pitch. Just as long as you can get it out between floors on an elevator – 35 seconds worth.
- Page is your gripping synopsis with no spoilers, but plenty of come-on. That is the base of your book description as well as

your one-sheet to pitch the book to distributors and buyers. A page is about 300 words. Learn to be terse, efficient.

Sleep, Rinse, Repeat

You want to read and dissect as many books as you can each evening. Then sleep with your head filled with plots.

Make sure to wake and write up any story ideas you get from your dreams. And rise early as you have to in order to get these out into our world before you forget the parts and pieces of them. At least do the sentence, paragraph, page treatment above.

Keep all these write ups where you can find them again. Printing them off and storing in a loose-leaf notebook would be smart. You can then page through them when your muse is "on strike". Also, if/when you decide to hire out ghostwriters, those will be what you hand them to get the story you want.

Lesson 5 Supplement - Ideal Maximum Production

Some general principles:

- You can talk between 10K and 12K an hour. Two hours of this will give you 2 short stories that are at least 10K long (a 40-page short read, each.)

- Four days of this will give you 80K of text in 8 short stories.

- Ideally, you have a major story arc for the entire set, which each of the individual stories are a serial which add up to a completed overall story.

- The output of each week gives you enough to publish 8 short stories/short reads, two half-collections, a full collection.

- Each of the short stories can be a thin paperback, the collections can be thicker paperbacks, with the full collection even being a deluxe hardback.

- Your audiobook should either be in two parts, or the whole thing.

- And you can podcast the whole set, and set them up to repeat during the year (6 times.)

But you'll have to work up to this.

General ideas on how to train yourself to talk your book:

- At night, when you are reading, read aloud. You'll be reading short stories to begin with, and books created out of serials later. Reading aloud helps you internalize that author's plots, twists, and language. Start with classics, then read the market leaders.

- You can even start by reading some of the storytelling classics, such as Mark Twain's *How to Tell A Story and Other Essays*, Marie Shedlock's *The Art of the Storyteller*, and Sara Cone Bryant's *How to Tell Stories to Children and Some Stories To Tell*. (These are all available on Gutenberg.org and are linked in the membership with discounts for printed versions.)

Tips on reading and editing your book:

- Learn the specifics of your particular program. Dragon Naturally Speaking allows you to punctuate as you go by stating certain terms after a short pause. Google Docs on Chrome also has these.

- Practice will improve your accuracy and cut down your editing time.

Lesson 6 Supplement - The Overall Editing-Publishing Workflow

General Story Production Workflow

The simplest view of this:

1. Write a story. (Speaking your book is fastest way to get to a first draft.)

2. Edit it into shape. Line edit (use ProWritingAid)

3. Post to Wattpad for Crowd-edit

4. Pull it after a decent amount of time. (And replace with a new story or set of them.)

5. Proof with beta-readers.

6. Add in your reader magnets front and back, generate epub with Calibre (or online with Draft2Digital.)

7. Update Title and Get your cover, description, other meta-data, and category choices (use K-lytics, KDPRocket, KindleSpy)

8. Pre-schedule to Amazon for 90-day window.

This gets more complex as your writing gets faster and you can approach creating 8 short stories in a week. The stories may overlap and tend to leapfrog as they are ready.

The optimal time for Wattpad Crowd-editing hasn't been determined. It might be weeks or it may take a month to get enough eyeballs on it.

Four-Proof Self-Editing

This is a work-flow which gives you the digital, print, and audio versions all ready at the same time for simultaneous publishing:

1. Read your book using either Chrome and Google Docs, a program like Dragon Naturally Speaking, Enhanced Dictation on a MAC, or record and upload to Trint.com and edit it there. (Or you can use more expensive services.) - First Proof

2. Edit this into shape the way you like it. - Second Proof

3. Run it through ProWritingAid for a good line edit. - Third Proof

4. Read this outloud and record it, making changes as you go. - Fourth Proof.

5. Send it out for Crowd-edit on Wattpad and then to your beta-readers.

6. Meanwhile, edit the audio into shape. Consider posting this as a podcast to start marketing it.

7. When you have the critiques, correct them. Re-record any major changes you make.

Publishing

1. Create three ebook versions from the text: 1) Draft 2 Digital for the major players. 2) Smashwords to get it into libraries. 3) Amazon version with any special tweaks needed.

2. Ensure you have a re-direct link in the back pages of that ebook to a landing page on your site that has the entire series linked to Amazon and everywhere else. (No ebook outlet allows you to link to their competitors – but they will/should allow you to link to your own site.) And if you have a podcast based on the book, make sure you put that link in there as well.

3. Post the Kindle vesion and maybe the D2D and Smashword versions on pre-order. (It's okay they show up everywhere else first, but you should take advantage of pre-orders in your launch if you can.)

4. Edit the print version into shape, export the PDF and upload to Lulu.com. Make ebook there as well (no pre-order possible) and the paperback and hardback versions. Order your proofs (take about two weeks to get back.)

5. Upload the audio files to Findaway.com to get them out to everywhere possible. The sales page here should have all the links as well.

6. When the proofs arrive, approve them (or fix errors and re-order proof). Once they are approved, they will show up on Amazon, ahead of the ebook.

7. Consider making a course out of the book if you didn't produce the book already as part of a course.

8. When the Kindle version goes live, update your "leave a review" links. When other books come out in this series, update the ebook again.

9. Link the print and audio versions to your ebook on Kindle. You have to wait until you get the ASIN.

Lesson 7 Supplement - A Working Guide to Publishing Your Passive Income Empire, Step-By-Step.

Of course, and as always, test everything I say and prove it for yourself. It isn't worth anything unless you can use it for yourself.

Strategy:

0. We start out with short reads (5k - 8K words) to test the market and improve your writing skills. (Note: this is primarily directed toward the Amazon eco-system.)

I. Setting Basics:

Start publishing in sets of four, posted two weeks apart for optimal effect. Assuming probably 10K short stories.

- First one is permafree. Has opt-in magnet to get the second book free.

- 2nd and rest are published at $2.99 (depending on length)

- Collection of four at $3.99 or $4.99 (depending on length)

1a. Paperback, audio, and CD are published simultaneously for each ebook. Published slightly ahead of that ebook. Minimum on CreateSpace is 28 pages.

1b. At 2K words per day, creating a book one week and then editing and creating a cover and meta-data for it the next will probably wind up leapfrogging your books so that your launch subscriber list has time to review each one before you publish.

Write well ahead of publishing as much as you want, so that you can publish a minimum of three books in a series, plus that collection.

Notes:

- Reader Magnet opt-in's front and back, which then build your list.

- FB ads can be profitably run on the collection to boost sales.

- Sales boost opt-ins to list.

- In theory, you could keep up a regular production of content published every two weeks.
- This planning is set up to expand starting from no books and a small list, if any.

II. Expansion

Start getting book blogger reviews and radio/podcast interviews on a regular basis.

- Seasons are set up in hardcopy versions to go into libraries as paperback and hardback. They just need a data block for libraries and accepted into wholesalers.
- List grows larger and Ambassador sub-list is built, in addition to Early notifiers.

III. Building Team

- Regular appearances on radio and podcast shows.
- Look for promotion opportunities with other authors you find on Goodreads and other channels.

The Steps:

0. Get into the Kindling course to better understand the steps below. (Link in Appendix)

1. Set up a blog that allows you to have landing pages. Start a blog or podcast. Get a mailing list service. Set up your publishing accounts with KDP and aggregators. Set up Goodreads, Wattpad, and LibraryThing accounts if you don't already have them.

1a. Start posting to your blog at least weekly – can be anything.

2. Do your homework on genre/category, keywords, targeted audience demographics. Concentrate an a specific genre and produce a series of content for this exact area.

3. Create a series of four short books as part of a series:

- Find a hook for the series and each book - 20 words
- Write a paragraph for each book - elevator speech
- Create title, description, cover for those books
- Plot and write each book.

- Self-edit into shape. Get them proofed.

4. If you have any people on your email list, get them to review them.

5. Port to Kindle a week or two apart.

- 1st is perma-free - port to Draft2Digital to make the others free, then get Amazon to price-match.

- Reader magnet is initially for some other cheatsheet or content upgrade.

- 2nd and rest are $2.99 – same reader magnet as above

- Then publish collection of all four for $4.99.

- Revise lead magnet later as needed.

- You can repeat the above for the next four in the series.

6. Start doing giveaways to jumpstart email subscribers. Utilize Goodreads and LibraryThing, as well as Instafreebie. Post your permafree books on Wattpad and leave them there.

7. Publish paperbacks of each book and collection before the ebook goes live, through CS.

8. Audio is created as part of editing and is posted on podcast, aligned with your Kindle schedule, linking to each individual book and collection Distribute through Findaway, as well as CDBaby.

9. All books are sold on your own site through their individual sales pages. Your list gets early notification and post release discounts. (You can give discounts here that other sites can't. Keep your list happy.)

10. Port ebooks to Smashwords, PublishDrive, and StreetLib to get into other wholesalers and libraries.

11. Get Global Distribution on Lulu hardcopy books to get them into Ingram. (Ignore Createspace and other Amazon imprints as they aren't generally or widely accepted by brick-and-mortar stores.) Until Amazon starts slowing acceptance of Lulu books, and preferring their own, Lulu is the fast and inexpensive route to hardcopy distribution.

12. Do at least three promotion activities daily.

Disclaimer

The author and publisher of this Ebook and the accompanying materials have used their best efforts in preparing this Ebook. The author and publisher make no representation or warranties with respect to the accuracy, applicability, fitness, or completeness of the contents of this Ebook. The information contained in this Ebook is strictly for educational purposes. Therefore, if you wish to apply ideas contained in this Ebook, you are taking full responsibility for your actions.

The author and publisher disclaim any warranties (express or implied), merchantability, or fitness for any particular purpose. The author and publisher shall in no event be held liable to any party for any direct, indirect, punitive, special, incidental or other consequential damages arising directly or indirectly from any use of this material, which is provided "as is", and without warranties.

As always, the advice of a competent legal, tax, accounting or other professional should be sought. The author and publisher do not warrant the performance, effectiveness or applicability of any sites listed or linked to in this Ebook. All links are for information purposes only and are not warranted for content, accuracy or any other implied or explicit purpose.

Lawyers are funny: Your mileage may vary. "Caution Contents May Be Hot."

Index

Online course and additional materials are available at

http://livesensical.com/go/author-freedom/

Bonus

Who Else Wants to Write Bestsellers That Become Classics?

Get No-Charge Access to
Writing and Publishing Materials
from Our Library Collection

Instant Access - Join Here

Click or type into your browser:

http://livesensical.com/go/writingbooks/

www.ingramcontent.com/pod-product-compliance
Lightning Source LLC
Chambersburg PA
CBHW021933170526
45157CB00005B/2304